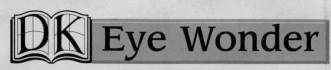

Whale
& Dolphins

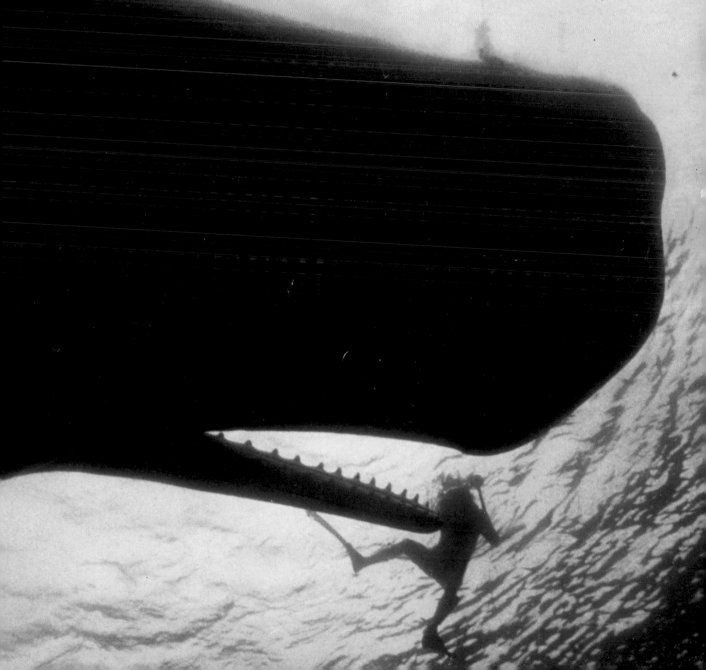

LONDON, NEW YORK, MUNICH,
MELBOURNE, and DELHI

Written and edited by Caroline Bingham
Designed by Helen Chapman and Cheryl Telfer

Publishing manager Susan Leonard
Managing art editor Clare Sheddon
Jacket design Chris Drew
Picture researcher Bridget Tily
Production Shivani Pandey
DTP Designer Almudena Díaz
Consultant Kim Dennis-Bryan PhD, FZS
With thanks to Venice Shone for artwork.

First published in Great Britain in 2003 by
Dorling Kindersley Limited
80 Strand, London WC2R 0RL

A Penguin Company

8 10 9

Copyright © 2003 Dorling Kindersley Limited, London
First paperback edition 2005

A CIP catalogue record for this book
is available from the British Library.

Paperback edition ISBN 978-1-40530-965-3
Hardback edition ISBN 978-0-75136-767-6
Hardback edition published as *Whales & Dolphins*

Colour reproduction by Colourscan, Singapore
Printed and bound in Italy by L.E.G.O.

Discover more at
www.dk.com

Contents

A mammal not a fish

All of the animals on these pages are able to glide through the water, but they are not fish. They are warm-blooded mammals, just like us. They have lungs not gills and must come to the surface to breathe air.

Breathe in
Whales and dolphins draw air into their lungs through a blowhole, not through their mouths. The blowhole is positioned on top of their heads

We like milk!

Baby sea lions, like all mammals, suckle their mother's milk. The nipples are hidden in slits on the mother's tummy. The rich milk is about 50 per cent fat.

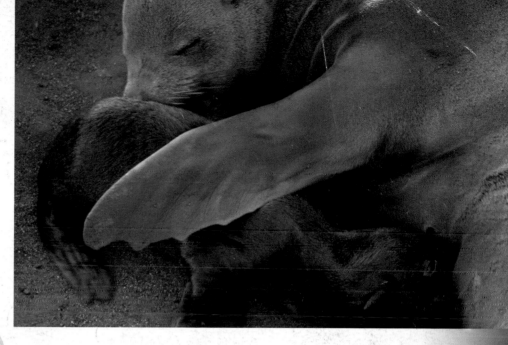

Whale's milk is about 10 times richer in fat than cow's milk.

Blubber for warmth

Many whales, dolphins, and seals live in icy places. Under the skin, a thick, oily fat called blubber protects them from the cold.

Sea lion's milk is as thick as mayonnaise. A pup will suckle for up to a year.

A baby seal's white fur helps to hide it.

Helping hair

Seals and sea lions have sensitive whiskers, which help them to find their food because they pick up on movement under the water.

As it dives, a seal expels all the air from its lungs.

Taking a breath

Because they are mammals, whales, dolphins, and seals all have to come to the surface to breathe. How long they stay underwater after taking a breath varies from a few minutes to about two hours, depending on the species.

Some seal species can dive to depths of more than 900 m (3,000 ft).

Strong muscles around the blowhole close it before the animal dives.

One hole...

A whale's blowhole – a muscular opening that leads to the animal's lungs – is positioned on the top of its head. Toothed whales, such as orcas, belugas and dolphins, have only one blowhole.

...or two

Baleen whales, such as the humpback, have two blowholes. The skin around the blowhole is very sensitive, so the whale knows when it is clear of the water and it is safe to open it.

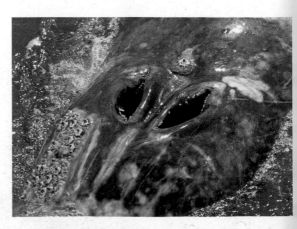

Going down empty

A seal is unusual because it breathes out as it dives, closing its nostrils and blocking its windpipe so that it dives with empty lungs. Oxygen from the air has already entered its blood supply, and is feeding its brain and its muscles.

A seal might stay underwater for about 70 minutes.

"Thar she blows!"

When a whale surfaces, it breathes out rapidly producing a "blow" or "spout", which is a spray of seawater. A large whale's blow can be up to 4 m (13 ft) high and can be seen several kilometres away.

Air facts

● A humpback can hold its breath for 30 minutes, but will usually surface every 4–10 minutes.

● Sperm whales stay under for up to 75 minutes.

In the 1800s, whalers could recognize the type of whale by the height and direction of its blow.

Swift swimmers

Whales are the sprinters of the seas, using their tails to power forward. Unlike land mammals, different whales share the same basic shape. It's the best shape for cruising through the water.

The dorsal fin helps to stop a whale from rolling in the water.

Dolphins live in schools of up to 1,000 animals. They twist and turn continually to avoid collisions.

Let's play
Dolphins have great fun riding the bow waves of boats and ships, or swimming in the frothy wake, jostling for position.

Built for speed

Orcas are the fastest of all sea mammals, but most whales are pretty swift swimmers. Their torpedo-shaped bodies are perfect for cutting through the water.

A short, stiff neck helps the whale to swim fast.

Different species of whale have differently shaped beaks. Some have no beak at all.

A stiff neck?

Some whales, such as the orca, cannot turn their heads from side to side as their neck bones are fused together. This is a useful adaptation to life in the water, allowing the whale to reach high speeds.

A whale's front flippers, or forelimbs, are used to change direction.

A streamlined body helps the whale to swim.

Left a bit, right a bit...

The large front flippers help to control direction. A dolphin shows how effective this is when picking off small fish from a large shoal.

Up, down, up, down

A whale's tail moves up and down to push the animal through the water, unlike a fish, whose tail moves from side to side.

Powerful muscles tighten and relax to pull the tail up and down.

A great tail

A whale's tail is made up of two tail flukes, or sections, which are joined at the centre. Unlike a fish's tail, a whale's tail lies flat. This is the whale's "propeller", which forces it forward.

What a leap!
The sheer power of the tail's muscle is shown by the fact that many whales and dolphins can launch themselves out of the water.

Listen up!
A whale will sometimes slap its tail flukes against the water's surface. It is thought that this may be a form of communication.

A whale's skin feels as smooth and rubbery as a hard-boiled egg.

Flying through the water
A whale's tail flukes are thicker at the front than the back, just like an aircraft's wing. It helps the flukes to slide through the water.

It's all in the tail

Humpback whales have special markings under their flukes. Every humpback is different, so scientists can recognize individual whales.

The blue whale's tail shows how perfectly streamlined these creatures are.

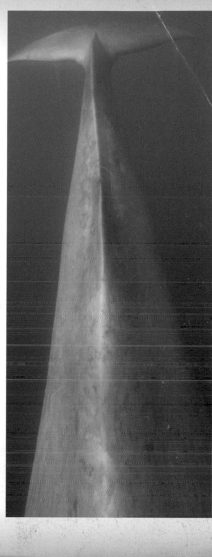

A whale's tail is full of tiny blood vessels, which help to cool the animal down.

Muscle power

Most of the back third of a whale's body is made up of muscle. The muscle is connected to the backbone.

11

Dancing dolphins

Dolphins form spectacular displays as they leap out of the water. They are often friendly to humans and can be incredibly nosy. There are about 26 different types, or species. One way of identifying different species is through their markings.

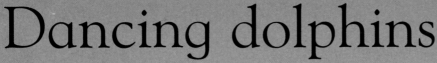

The dolphins take a breath as they leap out of the water, but continue to swim forward. This leap-swim action is called "porpoising".

Bottlenose dolphins can leap several metres into the air.

A friend to all
Bottlenose dolphins are one of the best-known of all dolphins, and there are many stories of them having helped people in trouble.

A porpoise, not a dolphin

There are six different types of porpoise – this is the harbour porpoise. Porpoises are very shy, and, unlike dolphins, tend to swim alone. Their heads are blunt, with no beak.

Spot those spots

Spotted dolphins are born without spots, but develop them as they grow. They appear first on the newborn dolphin's belly, and spread up.

The beak champion

River dolphins have surprisingly long beaks and, unlike many whales, can turn their heads. Both these features help them to poke about in the river bed for food.

A river dolphin has tiny eyes and finds its way using echolocation.

Scarred for life

It's easy to identify a Risso's dolphin – it is covered in white scars. The scars are caused by fights with other Risso's dolphins.

Risso's is one of the few dolphins with a blunt head.

Teeth

Whales can be split into those that have teeth (toothed whales), and those that don't (baleen whales). Toothed whales, such as the sperm whale or the dolphin, have simple, peg-like teeth that are all the same shape.

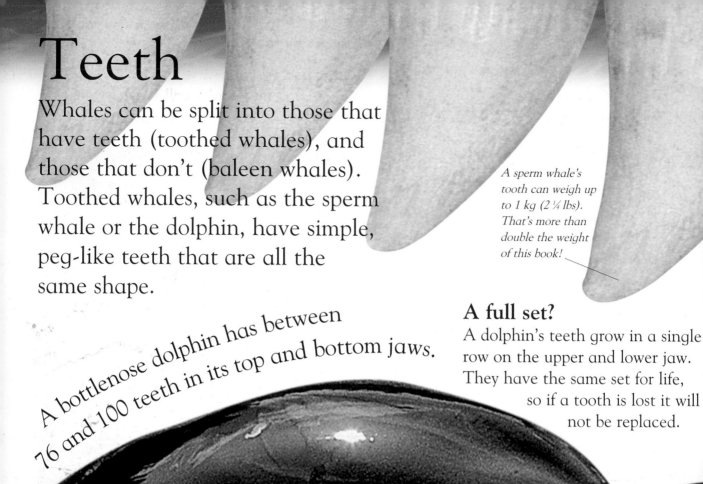

A sperm whale's tooth can weigh up to 1 kg (2 ¼ lbs). That's more than double the weight of this book!

A bottlenose dolphin has between 76 and 100 teeth in its top and bottom jaws.

A full set?
A dolphin's teeth grow in a single row on the upper and lower jaw. They have the same set for life, so if a tooth is lost it will not be replaced.

Whose teeth?

These teeth belonged to a fully-grown sperm whale. Sperm whales have the largest teeth of all the toothed whales. They grow up to 20 cm (8 in) in length.

A sperm whale only has teeth in its lower jaw.

The crabeater seal's teeth close to form a sieve that filters food from the water.

All the better to eat you

A seal doesn't chew. It uses its teeth to grasp and bite, and it will swallow its prey whole. Seals hunt and eat in water.

Not all the same

Seals and sea lions have a range of different teeth, just like us. This crabeater seal shows its incisors, canines, and jagged cheek teeth (which are adapted premolars and molars).

Canine tooth

How old?

It is possible to tell the age of some whales and seals by looking at cross-sections of their teeth. Just like a tree, one ring means one year of growth.

The filter feeders

Some of the largest whales have no teeth. Instead they filter their food from the sea through fringed brushes called baleen plates that hang down inside their mouths.

Big appetite, small food

Despite their enormous size, the whales that filter food eat tiny, shrimp-like creatures called krill. Each is no longer than your finger.

A humpback whale's baleen is about 100 cm (39 in) in length.

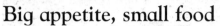

Humpback whales fish in groups of up to 25.

In the groove

Some filter eaters, such as these humpbacks, have throat grooves. These allow their mouths and throats to expand to take in tonnes of water.

The whales take huge gulps of seawater and food, then sieve out the food.

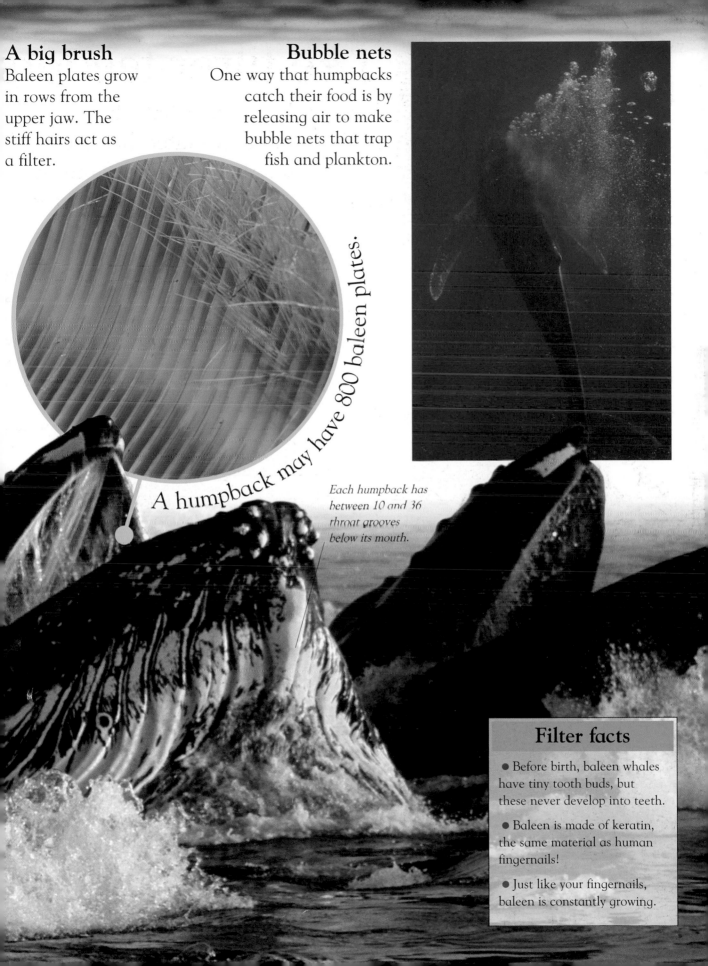

A big brush

Baleen plates grow in rows from the upper jaw. The stiff hairs act as a filter.

Bubble nets

One way that humpbacks catch their food is by releasing air to make bubble nets that trap fish and plankton.

A humpback may have 800 baleen plates.

Each humpback has between 10 and 36 throat grooves below its mouth.

Filter facts

- Before birth, baleen whales have tiny tooth buds, but these never develop into teeth.

- Baleen is made of keratin, the same material as human fingernails!

- Just like your fingernails, baleen is constantly growing.

Family life

Adult whales and dolphins are protective parents when it comes to the safety of their young. Many travel around in close-knit families called pods, and prefer to do their feeding in social groups.

Sperm whale mothers and calves form large nursery "schools".

Babysitting services

Female sperm whales live together in big groups with their young calves. When the mother dives to seek food, another female will babysit the calf and protect it from sharks or killer whales.

Join the club

The relationships built between orcas from the same pod last for life. They hunt together, sharing out the winnings, and care for each other's young, sick, or injured.

A warm start

A female humpback nurses its newly-born calf in warm, shallow waters. The calf feeds on its mother's rich, fatty milk.

Whale facts

• Humpback whale calves may grow as quickly as 0.5 m (1.5 ft) every month.

• If a baby dolphin strays too far from the mother, she may "punish" it by trapping the infant between her flippers for just a few seconds.

Sperm whale calves usually suckle their mother's milk for just over two years.

Sperm whales can live for 70 years.

Sperm whale calves are born tail first.

Always close to home

A newborn dolphin is nursed by its mother for as long as a year and a half. During this time, the baby hardly ever leaves its mother's side.

Humpbacks have the longest flippers of any whale.

Communication

Listen to a pod of whales, and you will hear a lot of clicking and whistling. It's their way of "talking". There are other ways that whales and dolphins "talk".

I'm here!

Slapping a flipper against the water's surface is one way of getting attention, especially when the flipper belongs to a humpback whale.

It takes immense power for a whale to breach.

A thick pad on the top of a dolphin's head helps to produce clicks.

Take off

Sometimes a whale will launch itself out of the water, before crashing back down. This is called breaching. Some people think it may be a form of communication.

A big argument

It's not unusual to see a pair of dolphins "chattering" away to each other, mouths open. A confrontation like this usually means an argument.

Bubble soup

The bubbles are a sign that this male humpback whale has found a female. The males also sing. Scientists believe that the sound helps them to find a mate.

These clicks help a dolphin to find things. It's called echolocation.

I see you

Some whales will rise up slowly to peep above the water's surface. This is called spy hopping. It shows just how curious many whales are about the world above the water.

A WHALE IN SPACE

A recording of humpback whale songs was put aboard the Voyager space probe in 1977 as a greeting from Earth. The songs are the most complex in the animal kingdom.

On the move

Many whales move, or migrate, to find food or to find a mate. Some make amazing journeys, travelling thousands of kilometres. This map shows some of the journeys that they make.

Which way?
Whales use ocean currents, Earth's magnetic field, the seabed, and the position of the Sun to help them find their way.

ARCTIC

Gray whales
One of the longest journeys of any mammal is made by the gray whale: this whale makes a round trip of more than 20,000 km (12,000 miles).

Many sperm whale migrations happen because they are following their favourite food, squid. Where the squid go, the whales follow.

ANTARCTIC

Sperm whales
Male sperm whales spend most of the year in icy polar seas. They head to the tropics to find females, who tend to stay in warmer waters.

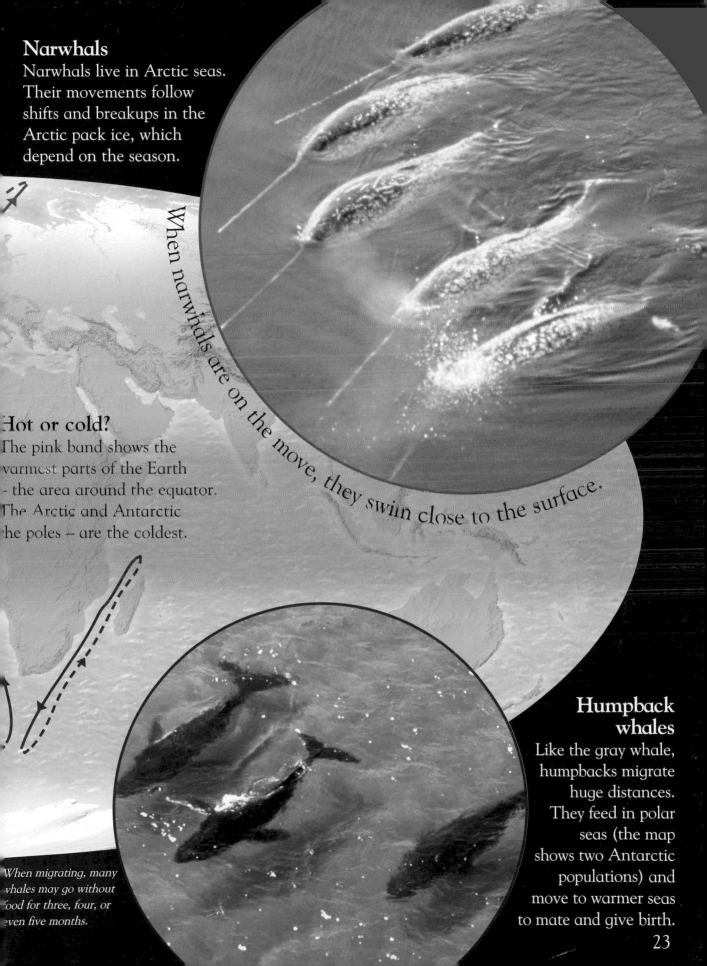

Narwhals

Narwhals live in Arctic seas. Their movements follow shifts and breakups in the Arctic pack ice, which depend on the season.

When narwhals are on the move, they swim close to the surface.

Hot or cold?

The pink band shows the warmest parts of the Earth – the area around the equator. The Arctic and Antarctic the poles – are the coldest.

Humpback whales

Like the gray whale, humpbacks migrate huge distances. They feed in polar seas (the map shows two Antarctic populations) and move to warmer seas to mate and give birth.

When migrating, many whales may go without food for three, four, or even five months.

23

JONAH AND THE WHALE

The Bible tells the story of Jonah, who spent three days inside a whale. An adult human could easily fit inside a whale's stomach, but it is unlikely that he or she would survive.

A baleen whale's jawbone is far larger than that of a toothed whale.

What a whopper!
The blue whale's massive jawbones are sometimes erected as arches. Here they frame a doorway of a popular fisheries museum in Nova Scotia, Canada.

A peek inside

Whale bones are more porous than our bones and contain a lot of oil. Oil floats in water, so the huge quantities inside a whale help its buoyancy, or ability to float, in water.

Hidden protection

Just like a human skeleton, a whale's skeleton has a backbone and a long, slender ribcage that protects the delicate internal organs.

Orca skeleton

Is it a dog?

A seal's skeleton is more like a dog's than a whale's. It even has hind limb bones in its tail flipper.

Elephant seal skeleton

A whale has a shoulder blade, or scapula.

Human shoulder blade

A ball and socket joint allows all-round movement.

Flipping strong

The bones in a whale's flipper are short and strong for efficient steering.

Finger bones

Finger bones

A whale has finger bones, just like us.

Human bones

Compare a whale's flipper with a human's arm bones. Both have the same bones, but they are shaped differently.

The wolf of the sea

The orca, or killer whale, is sometimes known as the wolf of the sea because it is such a powerful hunter. It hunts all sorts of prey, including small fish, squid, penguins, and sea lions. It will even attack young blue whales.

A large male's dorsal fin can be as tall as an adult human being.

Orcas, like other

Orca facts

● Orcas are the largest members of the dolphin family.

● Female orcas live longer than males. They can live for 90 years. The males live for between 50 and 60 years.

● Orcas will knock ice floes to try and tip seals into the water.

The orca strikes so quickly that the sea lions are taken by surprise.

We are family!

Orcas live in close family groups called pods that stay together for life. A pod can vary from 6 to 40 whales, and has its own calls that each member recognizes.

...toothed whales, show many signs of intelligence.

An orca will herd a shoal of fish before picking them off, one by one.

A fast kill

Orcas are fast hunters, capable of reaching 48 kph (30 mph) when chasing prey. They will pick out fish, one by one, from a shoal, and will eat around 250 kg (550 lbs) of food a day.

Shore attack

One population of orcas, in Argentina, have learnt to beach themselves in order to grab an unwary sea lion, and then wriggle back into the sea. The skill is passed from one generation of orcas to the next.

Deep divers

Sperm whales are incredible divers. Having taken a breath, they head to the murky ocean floor in search of giant squid. A fully grown adult male will eat more than a tonne of squid each day.

Going down

A sperm whale is able to dive as deep as 2.5 km (1.5 miles), though most dives are to about 360 m (1,180 ft).

A fully grown sperm whale is able to hold its breath for about 75 minutes.

What a big head!

The sperm whale's huge head is filled with oil. In the 1800s, sperm whales were hunted almost to extinction for this oil. The head can contain an amazing 1,900 litres (420 gallons)!

A giant squid may be 19 m (62 ft) long and have eyes the size of dinner plates.

Giant squid

Sperm whales often carry lots of egg-cup sized scars on their heads from the suckers of the giant squid.

Eye spy

The eye is tiny in proportion to the whale. Yet it is linked to the largest brain of any animal.

MOBY DICK

The most famous sperm whale of all is Moby Dick, a rare white whale in a book by Herman Melville. This exciting story follows a sailor who hunts a whale after losing his leg to it.

The gentle giant

Meet the largest animal alive today –
the blue whale. This animal is so large
that a bull elephant (the largest living
land animal) could sit on its tongue.
Other whales look tiny in comparison.

How big?

Everything about this whale is
big. Its flippers would stretch
from the floor to the ceiling
of your bedroom, while its
heart is the size of
a small car.

What a whopper!

At birth a blue whale is more
than a thousand times heavier
than a human baby. It will guzzle
about 200 litres (352 pints) of its
mother's milk every day. It needs
to. It puts on the equivalent in
weight of six five-year-old
children each day!

The blue whale can grow to

The blue whale is a baleen whale. It takes huge gulps of seawater and filters out the small fish and krill.

A shark-sized snack

A blue whale may be big, but its size doesn't stop attacks from sharks or orcas. This whale has lost a little bit of one of its tail flukes.

A big mouth

The blue whale's mouth is massive. Between 55 and 70 skin grooves or pleats run along the lower half from throat to mid-body. These expand when the whale gulps in its food.

27 m (88 ft) and weigh the same as 26 adult bull elephants.

Early whalers called the blue whale "sulphur bottom". Algae growing on its belly can make it appear yellow – the colour of sulphur.

A fat chance of survival

The enormously fat walrus may look ungainly on land, but it is perfectly suited to life in the water. A thick layer of blubber protects it from the icy cold of its home in the Arctic ocean.

I'll fight you!

Adult males will fight for space to be near females. However, despite looking nasty, these fights rarely result in serious injury.

A watery haven

The walrus loves the water. It uses its back flippers to push itself forward and its front flippers to change direction.

A walrus's tusk is an extra-long canine tooth.

Walrus tusks can grow to about 1 m (3 ft) in length.

Snuggle up

Walrus colonies are huge, with hundreds of members. It means there's a lot of jostling for position on the beach, but this also helps to keep the walruses warm.

A tooth story

Both males and females have tusks. Tusks are used for fighting, and the walrus also uses them to haul itself out of the water.

Fun in the water

These marine mammals are seals.
Although they come onto land
to rest and to give birth, they
are most at home in the water,
where they perform graceful
underwater acrobatics.

True seals swim by moving their back flippers from side to side.

*The short
front flippers
are used to
steer the seal.*

*Eared seals have much
longer front flippers
than true seals.*

Which are you?
Seals can be divided into two
groups: true (or earless) seals
and eared seals. True seals,
such as these harbour seals,
have no external ears.

What about eared seals?
Eared seals, such as this sea
lion, have small external ears.
They can also move about
more easily on land and
support themselves in a
semi-upright position.

Like many mammals, seals like to play. It's a good way to learn.

Breaking away
Harp seal pups triple their weight in the 12 days after their birth. Their mother then abandons them. After a month, their white fur is replaced by an adult grey coat.

Seals have often been mistaken for swimmers. Many legends tell of them coming ashore and behaving like people.

Which is the biggest of all?
Male elephant seals are the largest of all seals, growing to 6 m (20 ft) and weighing more than 3 tonnes (3½ tons).

The male elephant seals are some 10 times heavier than the females.

The sea cow

These creatures are dugongs and manatees, but they are also known as sea cows because of the way they graze on sea grass. In fact, they are the only vegetarian sea mammal.

Just looking for a quiet life
Manatees have paddle-shaped tails and live in warm shallow coastal waters, estuaries, and rivers.

Scarred for life
Because they are slow-moving, manatees are often killed or injured by boat propellers. Many carry the scars on their body or tail.

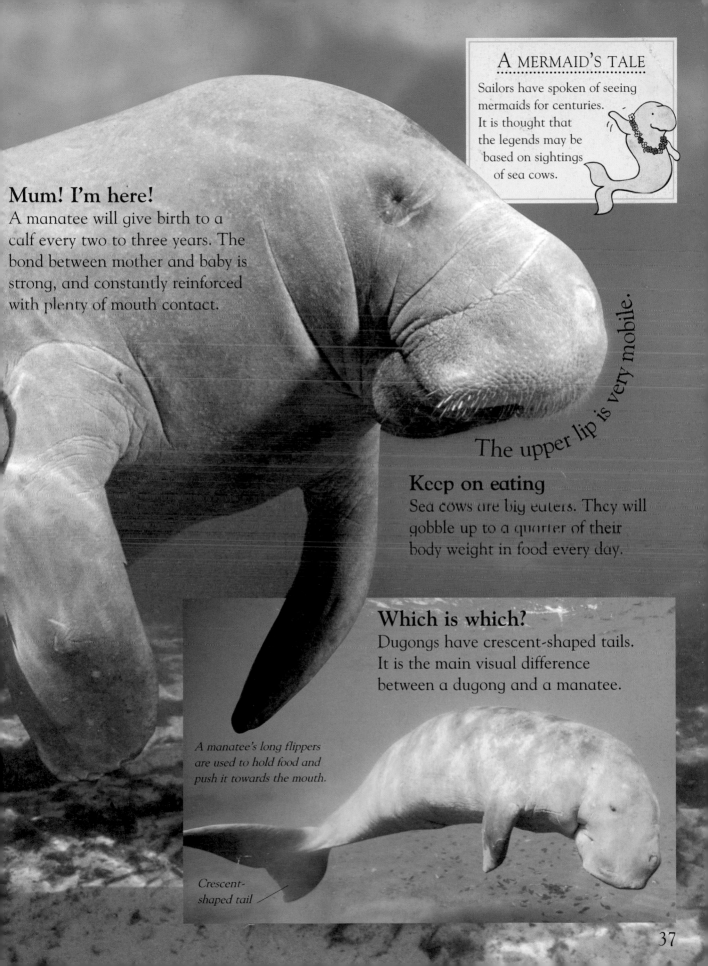

Mum! I'm here!

A manatee will give birth to a calf every two to three years. The bond between mother and baby is strong, and constantly reinforced with plenty of mouth contact.

The upper lip is very mobile.

Keep on eating

Sea cows are big eaters. They will gobble up to a quarter of their body weight in food every day.

Which is which?

Dugongs have crescent-shaped tails. It is the main visual difference between a dugong and a manatee.

A manatee's long flippers are used to hold food and push it towards the mouth.

Crescent-shaped tail

37

Weird and wonderful

Some whales look a little unusual.
The beluga is a white whale, and has the
nickname of "sea canary". It can shape its
lips to make all sort of sounds, including
barks, chirps, grunts, squeaks, and moos.

A colour change
Belugas are born blue-grey
in colour, but this turns
to white by the age of
six. They live in icy
waters, protected by
a layer of blubber
as thick as your
hand is long.

Tusk defence

The narwhal's long tusk makes this whale easy to recognize. No one really knows what the tusk is for, especially as only the male narwhals have them. Biologists believe it may be used in fights, so the narwhals know who is boss.

A narwhal's tusk always spirals the same way. It can grow about 1 m (3 ft) in length and weigh 10 kg (22 lbs).

Under a microscope, whale lice look like tiny crabs.

A large whale may be carrying as much as 450 kg (990 lbs) of barnacles!

A LITTLE BIT OF MAGIC

Around 600 years ago, sailors would return to port and sell narwhal tusks as unicorn horns. People believed that a unicorn horn had magical properties; cups made from them were supposed to stop a poison from working.

All aboard!

Some creatures make their home on a whale's skin. Baleen whales are often encrusted with barnacles and whale lice, which nibble away at flakes of dead skin.

Marine mammals

Whales and dolphins are not the only marine mammals. Sea otters and polar bears are mammals who spend an awful lot of their time in the water, but, unlike whales and dolphins, they can also walk about on land.

What's for tea?
Sea otters hunt in kelp forests for a range of seafood. They love to eat sea urchins, but will also munch on crabs, fish, squid, and mussels.

Sailors have long called sea otters the "old men of the sea" because of their white whiskers and expressive faces.

Sea otters spend most of their time in the sea.

Fur, fur, and more fur
Sea otters have incredibly dense fur, which keeps them warm. In a patch of fur the size of your fingernail, there are about 100,000 hairs – that's the same as the number of hairs on a human head!

Polar bears have been known to swim about 100 km (60 miles) in one go.

A polar bear lashes out as an Arctic fox, which is a land mammal, scoots by.

At home in the snow
A polar bear has hollow hairs, which keep the heat in. Combined with a thick layer of bear fat, they do not feel the cold of their Arctic home. If anything, they overheat!

Bear in the water
Polar bears are excellent swimmers, using their webbed paws to pull them along. In fact, their Latin name means "sea bear".

Sea otters spend much of their time lying on their backs. They will even sleep and eat like this!

The otters anchor themselves to sea kelp.

Whales in danger

In the past, fishermen used to hunt whales. So many died that there are hardly any left of some species. One of the problems is that the rate of reproduction is slow, so it is hard for them to recover from major losses.

Current danger

Whales are no longer hunted on a large scale, but they are threatened by our waste products. They become entangled in discarded fishing nets, and suffer from oil spills. They are also exposed to pollution released into the sea from factories.

Are whales still caught?

Most countries have stopped whaling, but some continue to catch whales for scientific study. This ship has caught a minke whale, and is pulling it up on deck.

AND ALL FOR A BRUSH...

In the 1800s and 1900s, one of the products that people wanted from whales was baleen. It was used for hair and floor brushes, combs, corsets, and umbrella frames. Its use gradually became unnecessary with the development of nylon, but it resulted in the deaths of thousands of whales.

What happened to the bowhead?

The bowhead was hunted almost to extinction in the 1800s, largely for its baleen, which can grow to more than 3 m (10 ft). It is thought that current population levels are around 7,000 – from around 30,000 in the 1850s.

The bowhead has the longest baleen of any whale. It hangs from the whale's upper jaw.

If a whale is caught in a fishing net and cannot surface, it will drown.

Save the whale!

Whales have been around for more than 50 million years – that's about 10 times longer than human beings! Everyone wants them to stay around, and there are different ways of helping them to do so.

Some whales seem to be as curious about people as we are about them!

Let's go see a whale!
Some people like whales so much they want to see them close up. This is called whale watching. It has become a big business.

A path to freedom
These whales have become stranded underneath pack ice. The people are working to keep a breathing hole open and cut a path to the sea.

Without these people's help, the hole in the ice would soon freeze over, closing the whales' access to air.

The tag beams data to a satellite when the beluga surfaces. Tag attachment does not harm the whale.

How can we help them?

There is a lot that we don't know about whales, including where they go and how many there are. Satellite tags are useful for helping to track a whale's movements. They fall off after a few weeks.

Glossary

Here are the meanings of some words it is useful to know
when learning about whales and dolphins.

Baleen a black, brush-like material that hangs down from the upper jaw of a baleen (or toothless) whale. It is used for straining krill and plankton from the sea.

Beak the pronounced snout that most whales and dolphins have.

Blow the small cloud of spray produced when a whale surfaces and opens its blowhole.

Blowhole the entrance to a whale's nasal passages, found on top of its head.

Blubber the layer of oily fat under the skin that keeps a whale warm.

Breach a leap performed by a whale when it jumps up from the water and splashes back down.

Bubble nets are sometimes created by humpback whales to help them to catch fish.

Dorsal fin the fin on the back of most whales and dolphins.

Echolocation a method used by dolphins and some whales to find food or obstacles. They send out a sound and wait for the returning echo.

Extinction the death of a species.

Marine mammals depend on the sea for survival. They can all dive, but must come to the surface for air.

Migration the journey a whale makes to find a better feeding or breeding ground, often depending on seasonal changes.

Pod a family of whales.

Species a group of animals that share certain unique characteristics.

Suckle the means by which a baby mammal takes milk from its mother by sucking a nipple.

Whaling the hunting and killing of whales.

Index

Picture credits

The publisher would like to thank the following for their kind permission to reproduce their photographs:

a=above; c=centre; b=below; l=left; r=right; t=top; Bkg=background

alamy.com: Bryan and Cherry Alexander Photography 41tr; Image State/ Martin Ruegner 12c; Heather Angel/Natural Visions: Tony Martin 45br; Ardea London Ltd: Jean-Paul Ferrero 23br; Francois Gohier 3r, 4b, 6br, 44c, 46t; Ken Lucas 39cl; D.Parer and E.Parer-Cook 26b; Ron and Valerie Taylor 22bl; Bruce Coleman Inc: Mark Newman 41tl; Phillip Colla/ OceanLight.com: 10tl, 11tc, 11tr, 11cl, 17tl, 17tr, 22tl, 31tr, 34bl; Corbis: Ralph A. Clevenger 34Bkg; Brandon D.Cole 20c; Peter Johnson 5tr, 16tl; Joe McDonald 35tr; Amos Nachoum 27cr; Richard T. Nowitz 24c; Jeffrey L.Rotman 9c, 19br, 29br; Ron Sanford 16b; Kevin Schafer 5br, 33tr, 33br; Stuart Westmorland 10b; Getty Images: 1c, 4c, 7br, 10tl, 18b, 19tr, 20b, 27tr, 38c, 40b; National Geographic/ Robert Rosing 33l; Greenpeace Inc: 43br; Hunstanton Sea Life Centre: 34c; Natural History Museum: 39tr; Nature Picture Library: Doug Allan 2t, 15tr;

Peter Bassett 35br; Brandon Cole 18c; Jeff Foott 32c; Martha Holmes 43tr; Todd Pusser 13cr, 39b; Tom Walmsley 8tl; Doc Whit 6t; Seapics.com: Bryan and Cherry Alexander 42c; Robin W.Baird 15l; Drew Bradley 21tl; Phillip Colla 30bl; Bob Cranston 8b; Goran Ehlme 23tr; John K.B. Ford/Ursus 39tr; Armin Maywald 13tl; Hiroya Minakuchi 26c; Michael S.Nolan 13b; Doug Perrine 13tr, 28l, 29bl, 29t, 34tl, 34b, 35c, 35br; Robert L.Pitman 5cl; Masa Ushioda 11cb, 20tl, 21bl, 48; Doc White 31c, 40tl; S.M.R.U: 15br; Still Pictures: Mark Cawardine 10tr; Michael Sewell 41br; University Museum of Zoology, Cambridge: 14t.

Humpback whale images taken under, and published according to, the provisions of NMFS scientific research permit 882. Phillip Colla/ Hawaii Whale Research Foundation.

Jacket images: Front – Getty Images: Charles Glatzer (br); Nature Picture Library: Dan Burton (bl); Winfried Wisniewski (c). Back – Corbis Images: Amos Nachoum (l & r).